NEW YORK REVIEW COMICS

PRETENDING IS LYING

DOMINIQUE GOBLET was born in 1967 in Brussels, Belgium, and studied illustration at St. Luke's Institute. Known for her wide range of artistic mediums and eclectic style of visual storytelling, she was an early contributor to the comics publisher Fréon's anthology *Frigorevue*. Involved from the start in the creation of the experimental comics publisher Frémok, she published several books with them: *Portraits crachés* (1997), *Souvenir d'une journée parfaite* (2002), and *Les hommes-loups* (2010). At the same time she worked with the Parisian publishing house L'Association and published two books with them: *Pretending Is Lying* (2007) and *Chronographie* (2010), a book of double portraits of her and her daughter made once a week for ten years; both received a number of nominations and prizes, including the EESI award at the Angoulême festival and the Prix Töpffer. Most recently she has published *Plus si entente* (Actes Sud BD/Frémok), a collaboration with the Berlin artist Kai Pfeiffer. Artist, comics author, and professor of comics and illustration, she is also certified as an electrician, plumber, and welder.

SOPHIE YANOW is a cartoonist and translator. She is the author of *War of Streets and Houses* and was a fellow at the Center for Cartoon Studies in White River Junction, Vermont.

PRETENDING IS LYING

Dominique Goblet

Translated by
SOPHIE YANOW
in collaboration with the author

NEW YORK REVIEW COMICS · *New York*

THIS IS A NEW YORK REVIEW COMIC
PUBLISHED BY THE NEW YORK REVIEW OF BOOKS
435 Hudson Street, New York, NY 10014
www.nyrb.com

Copyright © 2007 by Dominique Goblet & *L'Association*
The text of chapters 2 and 4 was co-written with Guy Marc Hinant.
*The author would like to acknowledge the support of the Communauté Français Wallonie-Bruxelles,
and the support of the Centre National du Livre, Paris, France.*
All rights reserved.

English lettering by Dominique Goblet.

*Cet ouvrage a bénéficié du soutien des Programmes
d'aide à la publication de l'Institut Français.*

*This work, published as part of a program of aid for
publication, received support from the Institut Français.*

Library of Congress Cataloging-in-Publication Data
Names: Goblet, Dominique, author, illustrator. I Yanow, Sophie, 1987–
translator.
Title: Pretending is lying / by Dominique Goblet ; translated by Sophie
Yanow.
Other titles: Faire semblant c'est mentir. English
Description: New York : New York Review Books, 2022. I Series: New York
Review comics I Summary: "In a series of dazzling fragments-skipping
through time, and from raw, slashing color to delicate black and
white-Goblet examines the most important relationships in her life: with
her partner, Guy Marc; with her daughter, Nikita; and with her parents.
The result is an unnerving comedy of paternal dysfunction, an achingly
ambivalent love story (with asides on Thomas Pynchon and the Beach
Boys), and a searing account of childhood trauma—a dizzying,
unforgettable view of a life in progress and a tour de force of the art
of comics— Provided by publisher.
Identifiers: LCCN 2022018884 (print) I LCCN 2022018885 (ebook) I ISBN
9781681376806 (paperback) I ISBN 9781681370484 (ebook)
Subjects: LCSH: Goblet, Dominique—Comic books, strips, etc. I
Cartoonists—Belgium—Biography—Comic books, strips, etc. I LCGFT:
Autobiographical comics. I Graphic novels.
Classification: LCC PN6790.B43 G627413 2022 (print) I LCC PN6790.B43
(ebook) I DDC 741.5/9493 [B]—dc23/eng/20220426
LC record available at https://lccn.loc.gov/2022018884
LC ebook record available at https://lccn.loc.gov/2022018885

ISBN 978-1-68137-680-6
Available as an electronic book; ISBN 978-1-68137-048-4

Printed in the United States of America
2 4 6 8 0 9 7 5 3 1

TWELVE YEARS OF CORRECTIONS

The Goblette told me about the famous day: the drunk reunion with the "fireman," the colored pencils that Nikita already had, "Bleeding," the chest "from when I brought back from when I was with the pirates," which collapsed, the Turbo injection . . . "Roger Out!" The whole thing, you know? The perfect scene to begin the necessary autobiography, and to attempt to arrive at, of course, the top floor.

It was 1995. The first pages of the first chapter were as impressive as they were pungent. Each time I saw them, there was oil paint modifying the pages. This troubled me a little, because I saw that black and white wouldn't suffice for rendering such nuance. Events transpired which resulted in the autobiography being put on hold on multiple occasions. There were other books, expositions, trips; the autobiography returned, left again, returned.

The method had changed: grey pencils now steadily rendered Brussels and Charleroi, but it was the same story from the pages of 1995, which, for their part, had continued to yellow. Reintegrating their sepia tone and their now-old style with the new-present was a way for Dom to defy time, the true first subject of the book, completed twelve years after it was started. This book smells of oil, grease pencil, humid wood, the disorder of the street market; it exhales twelve years of well-tempered promises, carefully untied and resolutely wrapped up. *Pretending Is Lying* breathes like no other book.

JEAN-CHRISTOPHE MENU
Editor of original L'Association edition

INTRODUCTION

careful NiKsKe

you're going to

CHAPTER 1

HEYYY!

I must be dreaming, they're drunk, they're dead drunk

We bought colored pencils but we forgot to bring paper!

Hello Blandine!!

Oh, isn't that nice! Aren't you happy, Nikita?

I'm not really, i already have some...

Hello Nikske*, so, what do you think of my new private parking spot?

Umm... Nice! very nice, very fancy!

*IN BRUSSELS DIALECT, THIS DIMINUTIVE OF DOMINIQUE MEANS "LITTLE NOTHING"

My neighbor loves me y'know!! He loves me!! I go out... he loves me he actually offered to let me park there!

You aren't afraid of dogs, right? cuz Kimi loves children. Right, look, i go for a walk, right, she sees a kid, she crosses the street. What an unbelievable dog!!!

YAP YAP YAP YAP

And my next-door neighbor... he loves me!

Watch this, i trade my "MOSQUITO TV" magazine for my next-door neighbor's "ENTERTAINMENT WEEKLY"!

17

YES! AND AFTER, IT BIT ME ON THE NECK AND RIGHT HERE, JUST LIKE THAT, FOR NO GOOD REASON !!!

Hey who's telling this story? ME OR YOU?

Next day, i put him down. Even though that dog loved me. Obeyed my every word. But one day he just went crazy.

Yeah well... this one's headed for trouble too...

I called Veeweyde* They wanted to take the body. NO WAY. COME ON! Don't mess with me huh!

* ANIMAL SHELTER

TAKE THE BODY HUH? way to go! VEEWEYDE!

HOW's about BEFORE we take him, you let us know he was a night guard dog in a parking lot and he was dangerous that they couldn't do huh !!!

Oof, Grandpa Mustache you sure speak baaad !!

Hey it's totally normal i'm Flemish

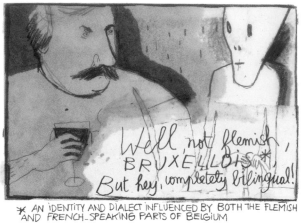

Well, not flemish, BRUXELLOIS*, But hey, completely bilingual!!

Fact is, it's because of that that i retired as a pre-pensioned CORPORAL in the firefighters!

* AN IDENTITY AND DIALECT INFLUENCED BY BOTH THE FLEMISH AND FRENCH-SPEAKING PARTS OF BELGIUM

They were ALL disappointed that i quit the service ... i'm tellin' you!

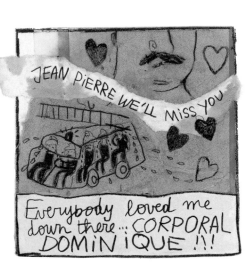

JEAN PIERRE WE'LL MISS YOU

Everybody loved me down there... CORPORAL DOMINIQUE!!!

YES DOMINIQUE YES!!

...ommy?

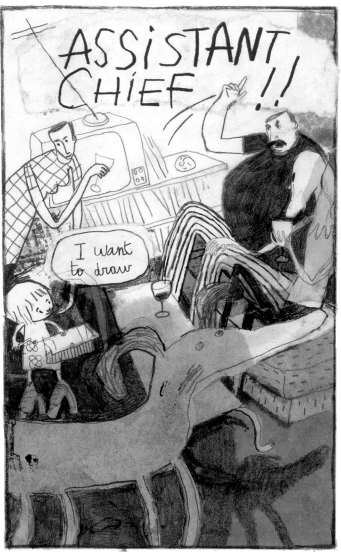

ASSISTANT CHIEF !!!

I want to draw

23

You Know she called me the very same day it was over with her stud?

That's what i'm Good for Huh!!

Anyway she always did whatever she wanted!

AND? YOU?

AND? YOU? WELL! Dominique...

YOU, YOU, YOU MADE A GOOD TEAM WITH HER

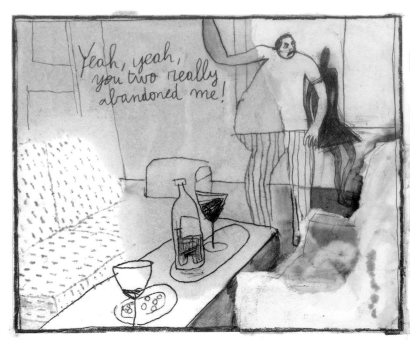

Yeah, yeah, you two really abandoned me!

AND i DID EVERYTHING FOR YOU TWO

I always took care of my responsibilities

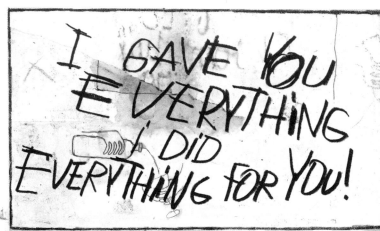

I GAVE YOU EVERYTHING i DID EVERYTHING FOR YOU!

I WORKED LIKE A SLAVE!! DAY AND NIGHT... did everything!! ALL... ALL for the two of you!

everything!

I DID EVERYTHING FOR YOU!

Yes well,

That said...

That said, that said...

Thaaaat said...

Thaaaaaat said... you're not gonna come here and get stuck up with me!!

Oh c'mon Papa, i didn't say anything fancy!

You with your U-NI-VER-Si-TY langage! Thaaaaaat said...

Yeah well what i wanted to say is that it's really the most basic duty for parents to feed their children...

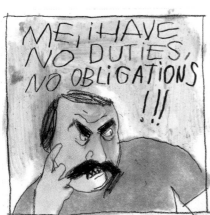

ME, i HAVE NO DUTIES, NO OBLIGATIONS !!!

Well, there are laws, aren't there?

NO DUTIES!! Nobody lays down the law with me !!!

Look at those arguments with your mom. I don't go through that anymore, you know...

Make no mistake huh, with Blandine too sometimes we exchange words

And then we each sulk in our own corner

But an hour later it's over!

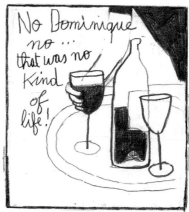

No Dominique no... that was no kind of life!

But anyhow, me, i've always taken care of my responsibilities.

And i was ALWAYS a good father!

True OR FALSE!

In truth... a remarkable father!

You know it's thanks to me you always had something to eat on your plate!

True... or not true?

Well yeah, that's true!

Yes Dominique, yes, you really abandoned me.

WHAT?

What did you say?

But... i didn't say anything

NO, no you said SOMETHING, don't be a smart ass with me huh!!!

NO REALLY i didn't say anything!!

I may be Kind ... But you can't jerk me around!

You think i didn't understand your little game?

Watch it, alright! You can't play that card with me Y'Know! YES Dominique, that's how it is and no two ways about it... I've got the receipt to prove it, YOU ALL abandoned me!

ALL OF YOU! Dominique all of you, YOU ALL abandoned me it's clear as day you all abandoned me!

But no Papa... It's you who abandoned us.

CHAPTER 2

Anyway, my father is above all a rational person

He was still young at the time, and was going with his mother to the coast. She had rented a house in Ostende.

During the night, they heard the doors and windows slamming about upstairs

He thought that maybe it was a gust of wind, he closed them one by one...

But an hour later, they were open again

This time, my father went up, closed them again and checked to see if one of them was busted

He was just back downstairs when they reopened for no apparent reason, all of them, one after another...

The dog got anxious and began to bark

Then there was a noise, just once, a muted noise, and the dog began to howl like mad

My father went back up, and closed all the windows again, for the third time. Believe me, he was really shaken up!!

He took the dog, it was a fox terrier and there, ... in front of a door, the dog stopped short!!

It sniffed under the door and its hair stood on end. I can tell you, that night, my father had a hard time getting to sleep

So he got up and felt his way towards the window to look at the dunes...

And it's at that very moment that he heard a sort of sucking sound ...right by his ear.

What are you thinking of making??

Sautee some vegetables, some rice, maybe a chicken curry...

Something good and simple!

That's all? You think we'll be done by tomorrow?

Wait, are you actually single?

Single? Yes, yes well I was with a girl for two years

...But now, i'm single yes...

You don't think it's... Um, a bit too much?

51

Too much? No, i love cooking ...and eating! don't you??

When my son is home, i might make pasta with tuna, for example

It seems like a simple recipe but actually it isn't quite so easy...

First of all, you have to fill a saucepan with water

When it's boiling, bam! You throw in the pasta in one go

And at that moment, You open a can of tuna! There are many brands. But in general i get "Starkist"

There is one with vegetables, it's not bad!

There are many possible versions: with oil, without oil, it's your choice...

And then, you see, you have to open a second can, tomato sauce this time

To know if the pasta is ready, you have to pay attention... At least, i don't trust the time written on the box...

...I take out a few noodles with a fork and taste them. If they're ready, i run them under cold water

When they're just about "al dente", you taste them, and you put them back in the pan and there you mix everything up, and you can add salt, spices, etc if you have them... and you plop it all onto soup plates.

EXQUISITE... AND FAST!!!

It doesn't tire you out to work like this? 2PM ... It's a bad time for work, do you know how many workers hurt themselves at this very hour??

Go on, get out, Mustache!

Someone called a few times ... But when i answer, they hang up! It's really annoying and unpleasant ...

I've had that type of thing happen, mistakes sometimes ...

But i seem to hear breathing. There's someone on the other end ...

Listen, if that happens again, don't pick up, let the answering machine get it, and don't worry yourself over it !!

Aghh!

I've had enough!!!

Are you okay? is it the TV station?

Honestly, i'm going to give up, i wasn't made for this...

Calm down, we're going to spend a lovely evening together look...

Listen, there are other things in life besides the day-to-day, all of this is great but really, it's going nowhere... It seems like i don't have time to do anything. I'm stuck... i do a million things and nothing comes out...

Ah well, bon appetit... nonetheless!

RAING!

ah... coming...

You throw that at me, and you dare to tell me we can't see each other? It's madness!!

Well me neither, you know, i can't take it anymore!! YOU should understand!!

Ah... is the tea ready?

But... That's all you have to say?

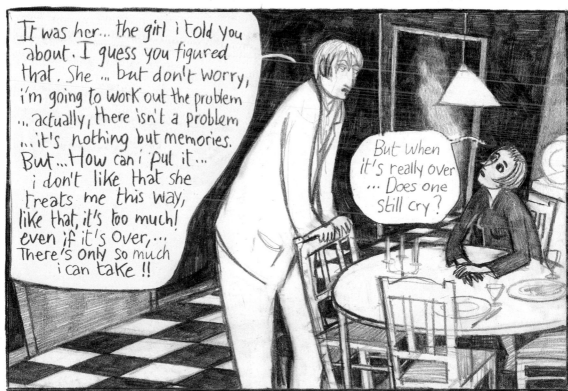

It was her... the girl i told you about. I guess you figured that. She ... but don't worry, i'm going to work out the problem ... actually, there isn't a problem ...it's nothing but memories. But...How can i pul it... i don't like that she treats me this way, like that, it's too much! even if it's over,... There's only so much i can take!!

But when it's really over ... Does one still cry?

no...

This hurts me ...You know i love you, but nothing's possible now...

I feel empty... like a part of me has died

You can't talk like that

I feel like my life is over, and i can't do anything about it ...

How did we get here? Why did you leave me like this, when things were starting to work out?

You must know, that you're the one i love and nobody else!

But then why do you live with him and not me?

But you have someone right now too. We can't always choose...

But look at him and look at me!!

There's nobody but you, you know that... we're the only ones who can understand that

HELLO, ANYbody home??

How are you?

Where were you?

Well, at work, why?

I called, you weren't there!!!

At the TV station? of course! I wasn't there... I didn't say i was doing the broadcast. i had to prepare it, do the preparations you know

It's not worth overdramatizing, what's gotten into you? what's the problem? Quit it for a second alright!...

I had an ocular migraine, i was totally blind for half an hour. I wanted you to come back.

You know what? we'll buy a cell phone that way there'll be no more misunderstandings!!

RIGHT, well, time to get to it!!

...But soon he feels responsible for the fires that spread throughout the city, stops everything and erases the recordings...

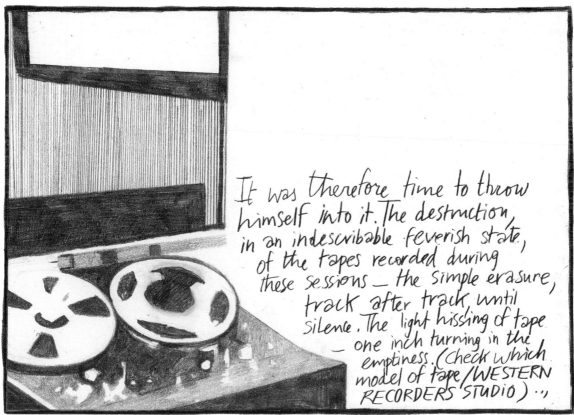

It was therefore time to throw himself into it. The destruction, in an indescribable feverish state, of the tapes recorded during these sessions — the simple erasure, track after track, until silence. The light hissing of tape — one inch turning in the emptiness. (Check which model of tape/WESTERN RECORDERS STUDIO)...

My work is coming along, but i definitely can't finish tonight. Can i take you to a movie? Would you like that?

What's with you? Do you know her or what?

What are you talking about! What have i done this time?

I'm starting to get sick of your stories, alright?

Woah, back off a little! i really don't see what i did that...

AREMBERG-GALERIES

COU

Take me home please!

Why??

Guess!

Well good timing, i need to be alone. All this jealousy makes me dizzy, if only it were justified!!

Can you please just take me home?

Three migraines in two weeks ... i'm going to go crazy

What's he doing?

Should i go ... or not? no i really shouldn't go ...

How's it going?

Not great ... you?

It's been five days since we saw each other, i couln't take it anymore, i had to come, i had to see you

What are you hoping for from me?

It's not for me to say, i don't know ... i'm suffering ...

The best thing is to calmly reflect on the situation. What do you have to blame yourself for in this scenario ??

Blame myself? ... But, he left me!

Yes, but what did you do to encourage another rejection? Because you've told me that it's a recurring situation for you ...

If i win at least one in three,

... That will mean that he's thinking of me ... Actually no, let's say more like, one in four

I really thought that everything would work itself out, but now i don't know what to do. I'm not doing well... I can't make a decision. I can't tell what i want...

Things don't seem to be getting any clearer!

no... it's true

So what does he want now?

He wants to do all it takes to get me back. He invited me on a trip... to Thailand

I have the distinct feeling that i don't really know you anymore

Actually, at least this way everything is clear. You'll go back to your little world and everything will be for the best

Shut up!

The time has passed now,... Something's telling us it's over between us

I'm heartbroken. You are the person who meant the most to me. I don't know what to say, i don't know what's going to happen...

Whatever happens, happens!

91

There's something weighing on me ...I have to talk to you about something...

What, what's happening? tell me!

...Your mother knows, ... Your grandmother knows, ... Marie knows, ...

Speak already! ? What's going on?

Well, um ...It's your father ...It would seem he's not doing well ...

...In fact, it would seem he's really not doing well at all ...

...In fact ...It would seem that he's in the hospital ...

...In fact ... it would seem ... that he's dead!

What? What are you saying?? people don't seem to be dead, we're dead, or we're not dead but we can't "seem" dead...

And ...Why didn't anybody tell me?

Listen, i don't Know more about it than that, but i'm going to look into it.

Come on Dom, i'll look into it and i'll call you this afternoon!

...I'll have a clear picture this afternoon!

RING   RING

?!

E-VE-RY-THING'S FINE!! He's not dead!! He was just in a coma but now it's okay, he's at the hospital, you can go see him...

93

JULY 8, 1998 — THE DAY OF MY BIRTHDAY
→ THE FIREFIGHTER IS DEAD

CHAPTER 3

But no Papa...
It's you who
abandoned us

ROOOOMM OKAY, WILL YOU STOP WITH THAT? THAT SOUND IS DRIVING ME CRAZY!

CLICK

CLACK

I'm bored... i never get to do what i want!

OH, AND YOU THINK i GET TO DO WHAT i WANT?

RRRAOOOOMM

GO ON, MAKE ANOTHER PRETTY LITTLE CAT FOR MOMMY, LIKE THE OTHER ONE YOU DID!

RRYYWRRRRRRRR

At my friend's places, it's at least way better and their houses are a lot bigger...

CLICK CLACK

CLICK CLACK

CLICK CLACK

CLICK CLACK

CLICK CLACK

CLICK CLACK

CLICK CLACK

UP! NOOO!

no!!

Aaaah

...To ZANDVOORT AND THE RACE UNFOLDS UNDER...

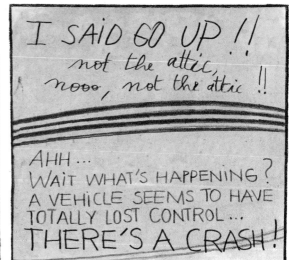

I SAID GO UP!! not the attic, nooo, not the attic!!

AHH...
WAIT WHAT'S HAPPENING? A VEHICLE SEEMS TO HAVE TOTALLY LOST CONTROL...
THERE'S A CRASH!

WILLIAMSON, IT'S ROGER WILLIAMSON'S CAR THAT JUST FLIPPED OVER...

...AND HERE COMES A DRIVER, THROWING CAUTION TO THE WIND HE'S CROSSING THE TRACK...

OOOOhhh, not the attic!...
SHUT UP!! ARE YOU GONNA SHUT UP?

...AND RUNNING TO HIS AID!

PUT YOUR HANDS IN THE AIR!!

PUT YOUR HANDS IN THE AIR i SAID! HIGHER!!!

In any case, i didn't know about this story about the attic... If i'd been there, Jesus and Mary, you can be sure it wouldn't have happened like that!

And... How many times did that happen?

Um... i don't know, a few...

IF i'd know that! You can be sure... Let me tell you, that i would've NEVER allowed that!

Watch it, let's not talk about this anymore, i hear Blandine and Nikita coming back!

Is her name "Bleeding"?

No Nik, she's named "Blandine"

How many croquettes?

I'll serve MYSELF!

She's like that! She doesn't like to be served, i've never been allowed to...

Wow, how strange! i find it charming when a man serves me. I don't know, maybe i'm a little bit "old France"!

OLD FRANCE! OLD FRANCE! OLD BELGIUM YEAH!

OLD FRANCE!! OLD FRANCE... I know what is to "be" OLD FRANCE!

OLD FRANCE!

Yeah, that's true! She comes from a very rich family and when she was with her husband, they lived in a villa like you've never seen! They made more money than all of us combined. 5 MILLION BUCKS.!!

Have you seen my wheels?

¡Injection!

TURBO!

180 easy !!

Afraid of a little speed?

Ah...nobo...

CHAPTER 4

We don't have these soles anymore, we can't fix this kind anymore!

Pretty soon I'll be blown away...

Dom? ... it's me.

Hello?

Why are you calling?
I wanted to hear your voice...

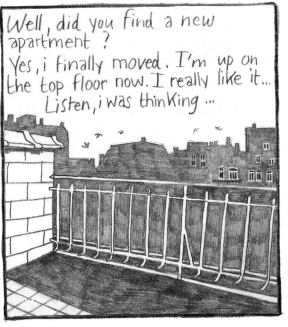

Well, did you find a new apartment?
Yes, i finally moved. I'm up on the top floor now. I really like it...
Listen, i was thinking ...

I don't want to lie to you ... in fact ...

It just flew off...
it seemed hurt, traumatized,
almost dead,
but in the end,
it flew...

I really want to see you!

When ?

now

BEGINNINGS, TOOLS, SIMULACRA

What does it mean to write one's own reality? This question concerning autobiography and fiction, already present in *Souvenir d'une journée parfaite** (which creates a fiction out of autobiographical elments?), turns on itself here: what part of fiction produces the singular event of focusing us on the key episodes of our own existence? We arrive here at the heart of the problem: how have we created, in ourselves, that which we consider to be our own reality? The past is fiction, re-memorization, re-interpretation, fleeting obsession (based on an accepted reality), projection, hypothesis, and opacity.

Our past carries memories that most often mix up what we have been told many times as if it were true (the recurring stories of our parents). How did we end up accepting this? They decide this is what will be our construction material. Secondly: what is my role, I who intervenes in a story that is supposed to be autobiography? Restructure, reinvent the relationships, so be it.

But what about my character? His disturbed and deceitful appearance only escapes my own disapproval because of this stepping back that is in itself the act of writing—it's indeed a character (composed of guilt, dread, suffering, etc.) that I attempt to bring to life within the structure of the book. In this way we become intelligible and unregretful. Everything can be approached without fear or remorse. Why? Because it is not just about life itself but about Art (the omniscient, unassailable power of art). This is why GM isn't Guy Marc and the Dom of the story isn't Dominique Goblet—these are, in reality, avatars controlled by living people bearing similar names.

GUY MARC HINANT

Memories of a Perfect Day, Frémok, 2001.

ACKNOWLEDGMENTS

For their support all along for this book, I would like to thank a great number of people around me, my friends first: Octave, Sanam, Zab, Julie, Sjakie and Hans, Pierre Hallet, Thierry and Eve, Bernard and Sophie, Martine ... but equally, François Schuiten, Martha the mother of Guy Marc, Barbara Stinglhamberg ...

But above all, I would like to thank my daughter Nikita. Her invested and attentive reading, her well considered comments and especially her affection have aided me so much. Guy Marc, naturally, for his incredible openness and the complicity that we found in collaborating so closely. K54 & Kulko Limoon from the UP Krew for their intervention and creation of the graffiti and tags in "Xa's bedroom." Thierry Umbriet for his visual interpretation of an ocular migraine. Joost Pollmann for the support, the attention, the faith and the investment that he has made in my work.

Finally, my mother, for whom I have lots of love and who, I hope, will consider this book an homage.

And to finish, Jean-Christophe Menu, without whom this book wouldn't exist, and who played a role which largely surpassed that of an editor and of an exceptional friend and who, thanks to his reflections and sensible questions, pushed me, when he had to, to rethink my work, and who allowed me to go all the way with what I needed to do, truly all the way.